The Audible and the Evident

The Hollis Summers Poetry Prize

GENERAL EDITOR: DAVID SANDERS

Named after the distinguished poet who taught for many years at Ohio University and made Athens, Ohio, the subject of many of his poems, this competition invites writers to submit unpublished collections of original poems. The competition is open to poets who have not published a book-length collection as well as to those who have.

Full and updated information is available on the Hollis Summers Poetry Prize web page: ohioswallow.com/poetry_prize.

Meredith Carson, *Infinite Morning*
Memye Curtis Tucker, *The Watchers*
V. Penelope Pelizzon, *Nostos*
Kwame Dawes, *Midland*
Allison Eir Jenks, *The Palace of Bones*
Robert B. Shaw, *Solving for X*
Dan Lechay, *The Quarry*
Joshua Mehigan, *The Optimist*
Jennifer Rose, *Hometown for an Hour*
Ann Hudson, *The Armillary Sphere*
Roger Sedarat, *Dear Regime: Letters to the Islamic Republic*
Jason Gray, *Photographing Eden*
Will Wells, *Unsettled Accounts*
Stephen Kampa, *Cracks in the Invisible*
Nick Norwood, *Gravel and Hawk*
Charles Hood, *South × South: Poems from Antarctica*
Alison Powell, *On the Desire to Levitate*
Shane Seely, *The Surface of the Lit World*
Michelle Y. Burke, *Animal Purpose*
Michael Shewmaker, *Penumbra*
Idris Anderson, *Doubtful Harbor*
Joseph J. Capista, *Intrusive Beauty*
Julie Hanson, *The Audible and the Evident*

The Audible and the Evident

Poems

Julie Hanson

OHIO UNIVERSITY PRESS

ATHENS

Ohio University Press, Athens, Ohio 45701
ohioswallow.com

Printed in the United States of America
Ohio University Press books are printed on acid-free paper ⊛ ™

30 29 28 27 26 25 24 23 22 21 20   5 4 3 2 1

Cover art: Charles E. Burchfield (1893–1967), *The Woodpecker*, 1955–1963;
watercolor, gouache, and crayon on pieced paper, 49 1/4 x 37 1/4 inches;
(frame: 54 3/4 x 42 1/2 inches); Courtesy of Reynolda House Museum
of American Art, Affiliated with Wake Forest University, Gift of Barbara B.
Millhouse, 1984.2.14. Reproduced with permission of the Charles E.
Burchfield Foundation.

Library of Congress Cataloging-in-Publication Data
Names: Hanson, Julie Jordan, author.
Title: The audible and the evident : poems / Julie Hanson.
Description: Athens : Ohio University Press, [2020] | Series: Hollis
   Summers poetry prize
Identifiers: LCCN 2019058665 | ISBN 9780821424155 (paperback ; acid-free
   paper) | ISBN 9780821440957 (pdf)
Subjects: LCGFT: Poetry.
Classification: LCC PS3608.A72278 A96 2020 | DDC 811/.6–dc23
LC record available at https://lccn.loc.gov/2019058665

FOR RICHARD

Contents

I

Real Life, Dear Voyeur, Real Life

Much has kept me from my task.
October has peaked here. To look out
the window is to lift from the chair
in order to get closer to those
leaves, still shining with the drop
in temperature, radiant with colors
too exact and pleasing to explain.
To look out is to leave the house
entirely, in search of a justifiable
chore. The garlic, for example,
must be planted, and soon,
lest the best of our seed cloves
shrivel away to no better than
dust-in-a-casing right there
in the box. And not only that:
we are completely out of celery!

I tell you, real life is a pull and a lure
and a fling-back thing, a need
and a need and a slow-motion slide
through all sorts of partially identified
coming-right-at-you sudden matters.
Some of them just plain practical
to attend to. And then, right before
Autumn, the yard was in Summer,
the whole out-of-doors bobbing
or zooming—at any rate, busy.
I hung our laundry on the line and,
charmed by the shape and efficiencies
of the wooden pins, was made
nostalgic for my own first toys.

3

Mushroom on the Lawn

What with a stem
so short, a cap
so long, so tall,
so disproportionate
and droll,
what with it standing
so alone on the lawn,
small and white,
nothing like it
anywhere around,
it was easy from the first
to resist the urge
to topple it.
One day passed,
and that cap
resembled more
a parasol
to shelter from the sun
someone pale
and imaginably small,
its silhouette
no less storybook
than on the day
before. But now,
at next day noon,
a bump's developed
at the center of the cap.
And the surface has
more experience
—with oxygen, I guess.

It's flecking brown.
If we are reminded of
our own hands
and our own arms,
we might detect
decline in this.
And notice, too,
the veil has dropped.
The cap is drying from
the edges in.
Furthermore,
one side has tipped,
giving us a glimpse
of gills without our close
approach or
stooping much,
visceral
without our touch.

Qu'est-ce qu'il y a?

Each morning my eye goes straight to the high bare branches
    of the ash
where a plastic Hy-Vee bag tugs and puffs
but has no choice.

Well I won't see that in France,
I say to myself, but the consolation is as temporary
as the trip will have been

once I'm standing here again,
staring at that bag
and thinking, Now that's the kind of thing I never saw in France.

It looks so orphaned and waif-like
against the shiny gray bark of the ash and the muted gray
    of the sky,
so white, so insubstantial, so wanting,

and, even with its one red word,
so caught there in the tree.
I'm certain it can hang on to the branch that has pierced it

for another six weeks.
There may be another bag in the maple by then,
recently freed from a thatch of wet leaves

or come tumbling
lightly from the garbage truck
that will have taken on that day no offering from us.

On the day we come back, it will still be
bare as scattered bones out there,
not yet the middle of March.

The ground will be hard. The grass will be tan.
This is so like me,
imagining,

not the cottage roofs of flat stones
pictured in the *Green Guide* to the Dordogne,
the massive ramparts for the great gone door of Domme,

but the day after—these littered horizons, and winter
still trying to get out of the yard.
On the day we come back

the ground will be hard. The grass will be tan.
But there will come a day much deeper into spring,
a day shady and humid

in the unfurled foliage of June,
when I realize I haven't thought about that bag in weeks
because I can't see it at all,

I can't see its branch.
The massive ramparts for the great gone door of Domme
will have lost a lot of bulk by then,

resembling more and more the sketch
on page twenty-one
in the *Green Guide* to the Dordogne.

They Are Widening the Road

The pipes have been revealed, enormous,
that lurked all along underground.
The clay-colored dirt is piled. Barriers
are fortified by barrels, hurdles, stakes.
Here's the backhoe making three-point
turns, the traffic at a halt. The heat.
The sun that bakes the dust. The sun
through glass that magnifies the heat.
Too near to every business here, and house,
a mile of road has moved from plan
to controversy to regret. Several
of the orange cones, disturbed,
have tumbled into rolling hazards.

Here is the church, the hardware store,
the auto supply, the bank, the gallery,
the pharmacy, the school. Here is the other
auto supply. Here is the world
with its six billion people, with its
how many random cancellations
of the single will, hopeful, defeated,
locked once to another—rhythm, scent
and curvature—in the ancient act
of increase, not thought of in these terms,
but felt: a direction that was sure.
Detained, detoured, deferred.
The personal is different than the whole.
We are directed into other lanes.

Does anybody out there feel
that the issue of fairness has been given,

all too often, a disproportionate attention?
It takes but gentle mention and the matter's
tabled yet again. With us
or without us, an agenda slips along
like mercury through tubes of glass.
The line is longer and the great big sound
from close behind is right inside our car.
There is no moving up in line
and the pavement of the lane ahead is ripped.

> *Pilot car*
> *Follow me*

Buttons

The sons of friends have learned to fold and snap paper
into abruptly-coming noise at my head. Oh, let them
in their red-faced rowdiness have a bit of fun at my expense,
I said to myself, what have I done so worthy of respect?
I've worked soil through a sieve, let it cover seeds I couldn't see.
I've taken pleasure in rolling up loaves of once-risen dough.
Yesterday I spent one hour picking free a broken zipper,
then spent another hour stitching in a new one to replace it.
Arvo Pärt came on the radio; it was easy to keep going.
Once I even sized and joined by hand six graduated leaves
of gauzy fill when I might have paid little more
for manufactured shoulder pads. Less and less
does my vocabulary match that of the television selves.
Less and less do I buy what they assume I have,
not to mention what they sell. More and more they seem
to speak and reach out to one another. I remember when
the newsman sat alone and looked me in the eye.
I might as well take one of the overlarge buttons
from my great-aunt's quilted box that even I have failed
to find a use for and strap it to my wrist for a watch.

My Job as a Child

I spent my childhood filling things in.
I spent my childhood thrown out on the rug,
rubbing crayon on pages

in big thin books
until color spread to the edge of the shape
where a black, pre-drawn line defined it.

I loved the August rhythms
in the action of the hand's edge against the page,
and the interruption:

the crucial exchange of one crayon
for another in the cardboard box,
one of so many decisions.

I used the point or, more rarely
(and peeled of its paper), the side.
I used short, quick, back-and-forth strokes

or long ones running in the same direction
or filled a circle from the center out
like the iris of an eye.

I applied greater pressure,
leaning heavy over my work,
or held my hand far away

and made bright or dark be faint.
There was the painstaking dotting-it-in,
there were curly hair strokes,

patches, zigzags, waves.
Members of my household
politely stepped over me.

The books were cheap and quiet.

One day an old friend of my mother's
came to stay with us and reminisce.

I sprawled out on the floor at some remove
from wherever they sat to talk, stuck
like a far star is stuck to its constellation,

and I colored along,
drunk in my deductions . . .
One.) Vi could remember my mother

from a time before she had married.
Two.) Vi had never married anyone herself.
Three.) Vi was an artist.

Therefore, for all of the days of her visit
I listened to their talk
as if any other action on my part

would make it stop.
And when one morning the story did stop
and Vi broke in and said a thing

that seemed to me abrupt and unrelated,
There will be no more coloring books,
I looked up for a clue in her face.

After a pause the story simply resumed.

A package came for me from Kansas
a few weeks after that:

pastels and paints
and two sorts of paper, one slick,
one absorbent. And I spent them all,

imagining a life of it, one thick page
after another,
bottomless, bottomless.

Soon only a smudged assortment was left,
and so I slid out the coloring books
and turned to a page

that hadn't been done
and began filling-in, no less satisfied
and no happier than before,

for the whole endeavor
was about texture,
more than we might suppose,

and less than we might imagine
a project of fantasy, autobiography, or wish.
The years have come,

and some few memories so slight
that they are hardly what they are.
They are agenda-less and dumb.

They don't notice that I notice them.

Improvisation
or
The Bluebird of Happiness

A bluebird came to a post of the garden fence time and again last summer and, in doing so, brought disproportionate joy. It wasn't a fencepost proper; it was one of seventeen six-foot poles rigged vertically as an extension to the chain-link fence to support a second, less substantial, tier. The bluebird preferred to perch on the pole mounted at a particular corner and reaching a greater height than the rest. Should that post become occupied by a second, less-frequently-visiting bluebird, the next-best option was apparently the pole mounted on the corner directly east of it, which had tilted a bit. I know there must be something sold at Lowe's which might lend itself better to the beauty of the whole while at the same time making the fence appear higher to deer, but we already had a few of these poles lying around in the attic of the garage and so put them to use and bought the few more that were needed. It has taken all these years for the bluebirds to land on them. But then happiness is often discovered close by, even if on any given day it might not register as such.

It's January now, and the temperatures in Iowa are about what you'd expect. Still, there's reason to go out. Just yesterday, having emptied the compost bucket into one of the bins behind the garden and having made my way back up the hill to the house, I stood near the side door, staring blankly at the aluminum siding, listening. What I heard was a simple choral accompaniment to the squeak of the gas meter attached to the side of the house. I don't know why the gas meter squeaks this way—the original one never did—but this replacement unit chirps at regular three-second intervals. I never spotted the bird and so can't name the species, but that note was deliberate, woven in, repeated.

Deleted Poem

It was good, but
seemed not good enough.
It was heartless
but throbbed nonetheless.

I will not willingly admit
how long I spent on it.
And yet it was easy,
once gone, to forget:

space lingered
but a moment, then closed up.

Time passed, decades did.
But it was boxed. It was hid.
Had backed off
like a monk with a hood.

It returned, of course,
disciplined, reformed,
as if it had, itself,
something to remit.

A Tan Dog Standing

I slowed, but the tan dog standing
grew smaller, not larger in the rearview mirror,
and farther not closer. The alarm sounding
from the tan dog stopped. The leg
stayed hurt and raised above the curb.
I had slowed with my brakes and then let up
and slowly I was moving on, and then
less slowly, while the tan dog standing
stared at my car growing smaller and farther,
carried off with the rest in the net of traffic.
This is not a street we parents let our
children cross. The traffic is intent
on something in the future tense, a flowing
toward appointments in opposing directions
that the tan dog standing must have wanted
to cross. I changed lanes but there was no
shoulder, no place to pull over or off,
no yard in a state of commotion and chase,
no house to escape from, where would I look
for an owner? There was only the traffic
surrounding, and a tan dog standing, tracking
my car with his eye for the length of two blocks;
although he was stunned, incredulous,
and had silenced himself, he'd struck a pose
and kept it; he'd stiffened with opinion.
The pain had been put and the thing
that was done had been done.

Why Do Men Spit?

I've seen it used as punctuation, transition,
as a substitute for content when there's a lack of that.

Paired with an action to be taken, spitting stalls and stretches
time by importance of the pause.

A man who spits in solitude has been talking to himself.

Some time before he died, I put the question to my father.
I could do this because I'd never seen him spit.
I could see that he was interested.

His face took on that focused look it used to have
when speaking with a man his age
—someone he was impressed with, or wanted to impress.

But by the time I'd asked him this, we were old.
I hadn't seen that expression in a while.
Eventually he said, "I honestly don't know."

I'd made him think; he'd given me as much as he could.
It was a good day in our relationship.

The Applicant's Wife's Rendering
of the Facility Tour

I-80   You wouldn't think of it, ordinarily,
              just driving down this road,
              field corn to the right, soybeans to the left,
              but dry ice is ice that never was
              and never will be wet.

Product   A sturdy box packed solid on Friday
              will empty by nightfall Sunday.
              Dry ice sublimes at minus 109
              and begins the mandatory journey
              to its natural state. Imagine the last
              gasp of carbon dioxide in the box,
              replaced by our common mix in a swift
              and silent exchange.

Perpetual   To manufacture it, they capture and burn gas
Reduction   that otherwise would have been wasted,
              extract the heat, and compress the rest.
              This extends the useful life of a substance
              and makes available to those in need of it
              a packable refrigerant. The processing
              is relentless, continuing on Christmas.

Precautions   Key complications are fogging,
              impermanence, and serious burns.
              Workers handling it all day long
              don gloves of polyethylene, a durable
              product, long-lasting, and seen again, too,
              where a partition made from sheets of it

walls off an area for the makeshift cafeteria:
seating, heat, three vending machines,
and a table where the gloves, clumsy as they are
for selecting a candy bar, often
accumulate. The Visqueen is cloudy.
The ice is opaque.

Options The choices are seen through lit windows:
sandwiches, kits of crackers and cheese,
coffee black, coffee with cream, pop,
and the seldom selected tea. The buttons are beneath
or to the side, depending on the model.
Food is conveyed through a chute to a shelf
or is nudged from display into falling,
there's a growling sound, and what is wanted
drops with a thunk for the preoccupied,
the dreamy or distractible, the tired.

Method

I do not set goals.
I move from bed
to the doorstep
where the news
awaits me, rolled.
The plastic bag
slips off easily,
the rubber band
resistantly.
I grind the coffee,
set up the drip,
push the button.
Wait. It's not
conscious, this
process—nor
contemplative
in the least.
Nonetheless,
from this start
the day does
find release
from its routine.
It's at this
point, I think,
that we'd
expect the sun
to glint
along the iced
railing of
the phone line,

the phone
to ring, the
heretofore
unnoticed
winter finch
come down fresh
from boreal
Canada
to lift and land
a little closer
to where I am
so I can
get a good
long look,
the wire to
continue
glistening
a while
above the snow
like it's a fuse
about to be
consumed.
Not that that
is what
occurs today.
It could,
but doesn't.
Some other
noticed
stream of
things is
handling that.
It's covered.

Squall Line Stalling in a Memory of Rain

A sidewalk begins to spot,
then the odor of wet canvas comes,
and peat. Oils on the surfaces
of rocks are released. Papers,
piled near windowsills or screens,
dampen into waves.
We are, all of us, solitaries,
sheltered in our columns of sensation,
and our columns of thought,
all else canceled in the pulse
of the rain. Hear that
whining, close and slow?—
mosquito, mosquito . . . a warning
too big for its event.
Now a restlessness is given power,
or perhaps just opportunity,
the particles and sounds
of here and now departing
for no reason that you'd
press yourself to know,
and leaving you instead
among a stand of pines so thick
little grows beneath them. And yet
the ground's transformed,
so springy under there and sensual,
it makes anyone feel young.
Somewhere in the north this is,
where roads are often left
unpaved, are seldom shouldered,
where seldom do you hear

therefore the surf-sound coming
with a car's approach.
To what then have you come,
leaving all the plants to drip
right up until you notice
that they're not: green,
glistening, suddenly sunlit—
as if the teapot is whistling,
as if the door is knocked.

Rundown Ride

He tugs my attention from the mill wheel
that works the water through the tunnel ride,
asking to go on. There's no line
and I nod and we get in. Although
he sits right next to me in the oarless boat
and my arm falls down around him,
he's alone. Even I can't see his hands,
he knows, his hands which he's been told
to keep inside, in his lap. The dark is only
broken by thin irregular seams and specks
of light that I misjudge at first as inches,
then yards, from our faces. My son relaxes
under them, a starry spray, a cool
mist in August. Our boat rubs wood,
one side, then the other, and as we turn,
the slits and dots revolve to the side and behind us.
As the mill cycles water through the narrow
board canals, our boat snakes by
three sights twice: the bear, the tiny Indians,
the farmyard—once close up, once a width
away. Gradually the ride has lowered us,
and in the end we rise, pushed into
the overcast outside, the bright collage
of passersby and booths of souvenirs,
the cutout billboard walls of other rides,
the line of boats he's made to realize
he must get out of now. He starts to run
the wrong way out, but is sent back
by an attendant. He wants to go on again,
he wants to be part of it, fastened to it,
his body forgotten in the changing design.

Eclipse on the Day of the Field Trip

There'd been an oversight in scheduling.
Our class was sent out of the farmyard
through a break in the lilacs and across the meadow

to tour the town first. Here and there,
groups of phlox stood in the grass and dandelions.
Our line relaxed and bloomed into clusters.

When they spoke of the eclipse, how long
until another comes, how long since . . .
they seemed in second grade, or first—years

younger than they were, and their guesses
gamboled over the century, free-ranging
and arbitrary, as if it were the field

around us, unfenced and flat, uncut by curbs
or posts or shrubs set at even intervals.
When someone turned to face the sun

deliberately—half dare and half
in disbelief, his eyes aimed under it,
then away—the sun was warm on our arms.

When the field ended and a cinder path
sent us east, we began to feel colder
and had quieted, our line more orderly

and closed as we entered town. Women
in long, plain dresses led us to the school
where girls were given dress-length smocks to wear

over their T-shirts and shorts and the boys
were given vests. These were kept on
while they wrote letters with fountain pens

and posted them, while they made purchases
by the pound, got a shave, served time;
then, after the talk about telegrams

and party lines at the depot west of town,
the costumes were pulled off and given back
to the guides standing pathside to collect them.

Wearing only what they had chosen that morning
without much thought, the bright and sloganed things
they had wanted once, they filed out of town,

guideless again, into the meadow, the class
of 2001. For what was there to touch
in the field, and break, to explain the use of

and the process of making it by hand?
It was near noon then, and colder. My skin was pebbled
and the light was lovely and the greens were lovely and wrong.

We ate under the shaded sky between the house
and barns, where in the rubbed-away ground
hundreds of crescents lit the dirt and winked.

In the outbuildings, littered with simple machines,
periodically our guide allowed
one volunteer to operate a crank

as the rest of us watched. And the one
whose turn it was grew serious, and older then,
capable of a multitude of chores.

An Errand

We were stopped at the top of our street
and waiting for green
when we thought we might turn
to the right instead.

I'd seen a cloud worth following—
more than a cloud,
a broad bank of white,
stepped forward like an army advancing

with a purpose undisclosed.
It was riding in low.
Development to the east of us
prevented our view of the whole.

A dark, gray, unindividuated mass
had pushed in behind it
as a backdrop and an element
to be reckoned with.

But then, too, those foreground clouds
were so arresting—bright,
distinctly lit, and separate
from the rest—

hard to say how much
interest resided there,
how much fell in from the context.
In the end, we turned left,

convinced we'd get another glimpse
on our route across town.
Which we did,
but by then it was different.

And we could see so much less of it.

At Pauline's

"Let's just stop by Pauline's
before we go on home. It's not out of the way,"
my mother had said, and so I found myself
standing in a room that led to the room
where the two of them stood speaking,
and a piano stood with the bench tucked tightly in,
and a television, shut up in its cabinet,
and a striped sofa with three small round pillows
distributed across the back,
and armless chairs, and a chair with arms
doilied where the hands and arms would rest,
and after a while I wondered if I should sit.
And where. Was it the phrase *stop by*
that seemed to prohibit it,
or this woman in particular,
her childlessness . . . I could see into a corner
of the kitchen where no one was likely
to be making a snack . . . but no,
I remembered then, she did have a daughter,
grown. As if she'd heard something then,
or been reminded, too, my mother's friend Pauline
took me to a small blue room
with a music box on the dresser top
and a View-Master in the lower drawer.
The one remaining cardboard disk, which later
I decided must have been the one to come with it,
was still inside. Snow melting off the Alps
came down to freshen the flowers at my feet.
Some elephants, stopped to grab the tall
green grass, green but dry and dusty,
flattened the grass where they stood.

Hong Kong was busy, crisscrossed with signs
and traffic, pedestrian and motorized.
I clicked on. There were no cartoons,
but toward the end, in a lineup of children,
one face in particular held my attention.
Refugees from the U.S.S.R.,
the caption said. Heads: shaved. Clothes:
brown and too large, gray and too tight.
Pump: gray. Ladle: bent. That boy,
second from the right, and looking
not at the pump and not at us
but between the two—which from how he held himself
was straight ahead—hard to tell
if water was a thing to him
worth waiting for. It looked as if,
today, he had his mind on other things.
I clicked all the way around and back.
That one, distracted, or about to speak,
standing fourth in line for the ladle—
I recognize him now . . . a prototype—
he'd turn out to look a little like my husband.
My arms dropped down,
my mother's conversation with Pauline
neared and turned a corner. The View-Master
and wheel of slides slid backward in the drawer.

II

Law

Like him, like our son is now, we were each
already on the brink of something,
and terrified. That's why we fell in love again
after our veering journeys—quick and stubborn, then long.

It was purely coincidence. It was luck. It was love.
We were falling anyway, which we felt by the speed
of our weight. We couldn't see the distance down
speeding toward us, but we were sure that we were gone.

Then there was a space of a certain shape.
And that shape was the one that wasn't fear, wasn't stupidity.
We didn't have time for further discernment.

We seemed tame to one another,
as important to grab as a branch.

It is unconquerable; it has

pulled down the branch of the far back ash
like a bow ready for release; it is a vine
so thick and strong it could be used as rope
on a steamer. It could tie down anything,
but won't. Instead it gropes where it will
and travels clandestine and thickens in June
when we are too busy planting the food
and the beauty to notice such a thing:
quiet, gloomy. Then it is August and hot.
We can't possibly take on a challenge of that
range and complexity. Its allies are the heat,
the humidity, and the four compost piles
of our very own doing. Its strength is its strength:
unmerciful, unrelenting. Giving audience
to our outside endeavors, it calculates ruin
in other quarters. The plaster has powdered
where a crack in the attic traverses the wall.
Mark its progress now, toward the aloe,
lopsided and loyal in the terra-cotta pot.

Summer Shower

Laundry flapping dry,
Dark cloud settles overhead.
Accept the compliment.

Toggle

I wrote two poems in my sleep last night. Or, they appeared,
fully written, and I had written them. I recognized in them
a better ending to my book. The first was five couplets long.
Hexameter, or lines of that length. I don't know what it said,
but it was no draft. It was an animal, born standing up,
licked clean and blinking. Complete. Then came the other.

It was just two lines long, and began with a statement
of great interiority. The line that followed could only
stare and squint back at it. You could sense in it the tilt
of a head, someone puzzled or thoughtful. Like a man
with large hands, large fingers and thumb, with an intricate
thing in his hands. He spins it slowly one way, then the other,
turns it over once and again, looking for how it is joined.

Re-entry

For weeks the central project was adjusting my pillows. I read
and sank. A trace of curiosity remained, just enough to turn the
page. I showed up for the food downstairs, although the aroma
generally unsteadied me. Nevertheless, I ate. Finally, I shed
the blanket and robe. My head cleared. But the sky was more
of the previous same—an opaque backdrop to a foreground,
dismal and bleak. Together they created a visual warning: *watch
your step lest you fade*. Odd continents of snow remained in all
the low-lying yards like ours where could be read evidence of
wilder lives, their deposits and tracks and their minimal thefts.
Everywhere something had slept, curled in its own warmth,
snow had receded, revealing the grass. I continued moving down
into the yard to the garden. I couldn't open the gate. The ground
had changed.

Advent

2001   A multitude of objects glittering
in the little shop, and from their various heights and corners,
competing for her eyes.
Not one of them essential, none of them
useful to this life.

1990   "And that's one objection to Christianity
worth listening to," someone told her:
"Not enough whimsy. Not nearly."

2001   But finally, she liked the ornate frog,
lines of beading running from the brow
on down the ridge of the spine and along the outside
of the squatting thighs to the spatulate toes.

A fly on the tip of the tongue.

2000   She would like for there to be
between the one thought and the other thought
a continuity that's greater than apathy,
and very different from alarm.

1984   Christ is a choice
full of holes.

1999   Night is the time of day for shoveling,
black where I've shoveled and black above me,
the stars static in their systems.

2001   Pull the thread through.
There are several solutions.
You're wrong if you run out of thread.

1999   If hunger for an ending
hadn't turned the page and read . . .
If a line were a dot. (Instead.)
Lost, spoiled, scattered, wasted,
otherwise attending.
Taken too far, on into mistake,
wrong turn, wrong ending.

2001   The choir sounded as they should, she thought.
Astonished by the Christ, and certain.

Dialectic and Infusion

> *Our thoughts are forming the world.*
>   —message on a tea bag tag

Inasmuch as our thoughts are forming the world,
let us control them.

Inasmuch as our thoughts are forming the world,
let us take off the leash!

I remember a time we were quarreling horribly
on a walk at an arboretum

and we were brought to a halt
by a surfeit of perfectly circular ferns,

the ricochet gone from the glade,
the dark peat, a buoyancy.

We Receptives,

we don't know what we are
until somewhere seeps into us,

self-evident.

27 October. Dreary.

When it finally stops out there with the fog and drizzle
toward the end of the week, the beauty will be over,
most of the leaves having fallen with their bright sides
smacked to the mud. And when one day of sun
peels them apart and sends them off with the least
suggestion of the air, where can they turn then, but back
upon themselves and back to ground, their vibrancies leaching,
their canvases swissed, then laced, then skeletalized
under the traffic of squirrels and shoes and tires?

We will come inside for color: the warm yellow of the lamp,
the beef-colored beef au jus-ing on the once
white platter, the squash with its sliding pat of butter,
the bright kernels of corn, burgundy disks of beets.
This is the season for deciding to marry.
The outside world has abandoned us.
We can feel it growing colder, and we know about
the landscape to come, abstract and simplified by ice.
It's another kind of beauty, a perfect kind of beauty.
It can't quite include us.

Passage Through

I'd returned to bed in the middle of the night and now my heart
was charging, my breastplate was being rammed, and what
was that all about I wanted to know, but my husband,
who was sleeping placidly beside me, wouldn't be able to
explain it any better than I could. So I let him be.
Eventually I fell back to sleep again, and I did wake up,
heartbeat normalized. Then we had the change from Daylight
Savings Time to Standard. It was two days after that, around
2 p.m., that I had my incident with the doe in our backyard.

You need to know first that two years ago last May, and also,
as it happens, around two in the afternoon, a newborn fawn
I'd discovered at the edge of the woods just beyond our yard
allowed me four photographs, allowed me close enough to
notice in her fur a smear of blood, and allowed me, further,
the gesture of bending to the side to confirm that's what it was
—presumably a bit of residue from birth. Then, remarkably,
she stepped up to me and pressed against and sniffed the thin
and now ridiculous seersucker material covering my shin,
and, even though I backed away before I turned, proceeded to
follow me: around the garden, up the hill, and right up onto
the noisy brickwork of our patio. She stayed for the night
in a bed of flowers. I was told by someone who seemed to know
that our yard would for the foreseeable future be considered
a safe place now; we were apt to see more of her. Which twice
before we'd thought we had—it's hard to be sure, though.
They grow up so fast!
                              This time she'd brought her young.

There were two of them. And the buck was there, too,
with his broad rack. They spent a good while in the yard,

the young and the doe grazing, the buck looking sovereign,
watchful, and snorting now and then. I'd settled on the patio
to read in the sun, so warm for November, but when I'd seen them
I'd set the book aside. They moved at leisure over our lawns
and briefly back into the woods where it was hard to sort them
now from the underbrush—their coats had turned—and so
I heard them, first, as disturbances. The leaves.

The doe came to the pear tree down near the garden
and turned toward me, stared straight at me,
then lowered her head, quite deliberately
and brought it up again, a nod. I nodded back.
She nodded again. I nodded back. This went on.
The nods became lower, deeper—so much so that
I realized what she was doing now was bowing.
I bowed back. This went on, even for some time
after one of her young had moved on, traveling south
and toward a ravine that leads to the park. But at last
she dashed off, too, through the fallen leaves, and, soon after,
but keeping a good margin between them, the buck.
I read a few vignettes in *We the Animals*
by Justin Torres. Then they crashed back through the leaves,
crossing our yard northward, over and down and back up
a neighbor's hill. I read a while longer. When I looked up again
I couldn't see them. I stood, and found them, then, in the valley.
The doe turned and approached me until we were level,
and there began another series of nods and bows,
which I returned. The buck stood farther back,
observing us with interest. One of the young had headed
for the woods. The other browsed in the valley.

As my head was lowering once again, the buck—had I really
seen this?—bowed his head and brought it up—
but it happened, if it did, peripherally, and seemed so unlikely,
too, that I wasn't sure I'd got it right. Except for this:
that the doe bowed one more time and then in unison

they left, done with what they'd come for. Their speed was swift,
their direction understood. Two days have passed since then
and all our hopes are down and devastated here
from the results of yesterday's election. Whether we sit
with it or stand, we keep saying that we're *stunned*;
we *can't believe it*. We mean by that that this
is not a consequence we can dismiss with grumblings
or sharpen up our irony and wit to help us disregard.
We have to face it plainly, and check our footing
as we look on it, and look more deeply, asking
What is this? And *What are you—am I—then?*
In truth, I don't believe we do know what we are.

I think I am a pool of bewilderment, grown local.
Like you, I am at best a pulse of curiosity. At best, I say,
but not across-the-board and always. Not enough.
For instance, many of our millions know to close
each yoga class with *Namaste*, and at that time—
bodies spent, breathing slowed, every limb relaxed—
it's understood this phrase is meaningless unless
it is applied to each of us. But tell me who among us
acts accordingly. Even as we push through the door into
the locker room to change, we are turned back to what
we were. All it takes is something overheard—
one woman to another, say, post-body-pump, about all
that she puts up with every day, and, from her friend
an in-kind remark about the meeting coming up, and *Namaste*
downshifts into something less as best it can. A wish,
a *there-you-go*, a *you go, girl*, an *I-know-what-you-mean*.
A smiling face pops in in lieu of text: emoji,
sunny emblem that it is, high-lit with gold, with orange,
still thrilled to be the new abbreviation.
A cirrus cloud thins to full dissolve.

November 2016

44

The Meeting

Four to a table. Round tables, so that some
must turn away to see the president speaking
and are at a disadvantage when it comes
to finding what they want in the pages on their laps and knees.
Most noticeable here is the hair, the thick and just-cut
hair the women speak out from and beneath,
and the various valid ways to have it fixed this year.
Pens are rummaged from purses and coffee percolates
in back, near the cut-up cake. And it's from back there,
after a report and closing joke from the treasurer,
that the newcomer makes a suggestion the president
doesn't hear until it is said again a measure
louder. No less than six looks exchange, quick
and taut, between new and past committee chairs—
Out of order, Out of order! Overslept!
—but they let her talk on, uncorrected.
Turning back to the matter, then, that they once were
speaking of, is done in the upper torso and head
of each woman. Like a key. As her father would.

Away

1. I discovered that I liked best riflery, archery, and fencing. Notice that none of these involve cooperation. And none involve controlling a large animal between your legs.

2. Three years earlier, at a completely different camp, favorite activities had been: 1.) complaining to other girls about other girls, and 2.) revealing the details of my life so that they stood in relief.

3. Camp is a place to discover what doesn't work and is not worth repeating.

4. No one believed me that there was a bee nearby, buzzing. Not until that one girl, I swore I would never forget her name but I have, looked into my ear and found the culprit cradled there, removed him and was stung doing so. She became my dear friend until the end of camp. What was her name, what was her name? That I loved her may have been due more to the fact that she believed me enough to look than that she had saved me from the sting of the bee.

5. Years later, once I had finally been stung, I felt ridiculous about my terror—all those spoiled outings! The bee sting was my inoculation. Henceforth I could exit into Nature unafraid.

6. The Dining Hall presented the communal life. There we received, we suffered, and consciousness was lifted into other realms: jocular, revelatory, mean. I cleaned my plate.

7. I noticed the flowers, although I did not know their names. Now I imagine them: Queen Anne's lace, coneflower, statice.

8. I knew the pod of the milkweed. Fluff in a harsh goose-bumped husk.

9. These became beloved: a photo of my dog, a pair of plaid shorts, a deck of cards. I relied a great deal on the deck of cards.

10. I was glad not to look upon the golf course. The quiet men passing through in small groups, stopping, bending down, slicing the air, moving on. Not until I returned home did I know it, though, nor how differently I'd view the greens, the rough, the little lakes and tees.

11. I liked so much the spartan look of my cot, the wool blanket tucked in around it, the foot locker underneath.

12. Rain: Chinese checkers, crafts, tidying up the tent. Thunder, and a plot developed.

13. Mail call: my mother's life made for unsatisfying reading.

14. Mail call: still, a wave of anticipation renewed itself again and again.

15. Suspicion: the component parts far surpassed the basic list: hull, tiller, rudder, mainsail, mast, boom, jib, and keel; every damn board and peg had something it was called. How jarring it was to wonder if this might be a concerted trick, if there might not be something below board about prerequisites.

16. To feel alone. To feel exhilaration.

17. To lack routine. To feel the new speed.

The Clacklet

Buttons taken from a sewing box
now mine, a little time to choose the best,
a doubled length of twine

to thread them with and tie up end to end . . .
but no, that doesn't capture it.
A bracelet of no worth,

settled on a surface in a slump.
That's all it was, all it might have seemed,
initially, to be

between those episodes ahead
and when it was the nameless thing I'd made
imagining the need—

a plaything in the hand, a teething ring,
a rosary for one too young to want
or understand a prayer.

It was a made-up thing
made up from things on hand,
and yet—Dependable Charm!—

it consisted of nothing but its task—
a guardian on guard,
and dutiful to every call,

until, left behind on the seat of a jet,
it flew from us forever.
Lost in the prime of its usefulness.

Forget something like that once
and it's not gone,
but churns around inside the void,

resurfacing and glimpsed again,
a referent for future fights,
little red sock

in a load of whites,
its status risen suddenly
to Item Made As It Could Be

Only By Myself,
lucky owner of a box
belonging once to someone else

whose buttons were all oversized,
some still shiny bright
and fastened to their cards,

who parked her needles side by side
each picking up one stitch's worth—
one tiny bite—of a soft, pink,

oval scrap of cloth,
whose measuring tape stayed wound
and wound inside itself so long

there was no true undoing it to flat,
whose sectioned trays
had organized like sectioned drawers

for years and years
a century's mostly ordinary buttons
which I had sorted through and culled

to make this simple, necessary thing,
an accessory itself,
now clumped among our losses.

If we still had it, though —
by now it would be
tucked into a box of infant things

and shoved way back behind
oh, rows of boxes moved in since.
The day would come —

we all know this —
when I would open it and with
the shriek of lost acquaintances

bring you running up the steps
so much lighter than I thought you could
and bring as well

our now-grown son, come home again
and curious about the contents of
a long-unregarded box.

And then would come the telling:
how quickly it had risen
up the list of what to pack,

how it had traveled everywhere with us
so there'd be no wailing, no regret,
and how it came to be

"The Clacklet" as he had learned to talk
—if, that is, we'd kept it
long enough for him to name it that.

How can I forgive the loss,
remembering now my anger over it.
There were other objects, yes—

but in only this
we get the bonus of a thing
forgotten famously by one of us.

Inscrutable detail, so well-preserved,
it hasn't sunk or softened,
shrunk, dissolved, or lost

significance for me.
Despite the dark bureaucracies
of memory, it is easily

retrieved. But you—
who from the looks of it
will remain my companion

to the last—you are the best
at forgetting what never came to pass.
It did work well, and at no cost,

but as a much-relied-on thing
its destiny was oblivion.
Had it not been left on the seat of the jet,

then in the upset of a different departure
it would have slipped
through a slot in the bench at the park

or stayed in a dip in the sand at the beach
and who knows how quickly
after that—a year, or maybe

only months would pass—before
he'd lost his name for it, The Clacklet,
if he had named it that.

The Prints from Vacation Are Back

Less than two months later, the name of the lighthouse,
the name of the cape are gone.
But here comes the ocean, giving a taste to the air,
giving long sound and seaweed to the rocks.
I walked the surfaces of some of the rocks.
I picked one warm one up and held it
three ways in my hand. Pointed my son to the gulls.
"Wasn't that in Maine?" we'll ask. "And the lighthouse,
did it stand to the left of the rocks where we walked?"
The photo before this was taken in a diner
in the rain outside of Boston,
an old steel one, polished up, each booth
with its juke box and out-of-order sign.
Blueberry muffins, reheated on the grill.
We were there so briefly, for tea,
on the way to Portland, where we stayed three days,
and where a pylon in the harbor a yard off the pier
has my penny on it, among a dozen others,
and a nickel each from my husband and son.
Before these we had added to the some hundred
not pictured, spent under water.

Daylight

When people are first born they look like
they've recently failed. They come covered
in blood and shrieking. Even their skin
is disheveled, their hair's a wet mess.
With any luck, the mother isn't interested
in that. She gives no thought to a life
previous to this one, the one nested
on her stomach and propped up. She cares
to be held long in its unblinking eyes.

Your next best chance is in the stranger's face.
Better put away your hand-held device.
You may never know how your mother
felt about you all those years ago.
You may never get it right with the people
you're related to. The bricks on the street
are glistening and the clouds are high.

Final Moments, Summer School

[In free verse] Nothing can't happen — and it needs to.
—Glyn Maxwell

The school and yard were still,
the yellow bricks and sidewalks,
the black asphalt they would cross
in all their colors, too hot to watch.
Beside me, in the front seat,
the dog panted in hot monotony,
although I'd been lucky and parked
in the dark vicinity of a tree.
The jay called our eyes away
and the unnatural cat, as smooth
and white as porcelain, fastened
our attention to the tree,
where action was just then
arrested. It was the lone
tree in the yard, a low-crotched
maple that held the cat
however far it tested, and the jay
came down from the upper branches,
came down at the cat
repeatedly — crabbing and claiming
—scraping like machinery
released badly on concrete.
And then often one was still,
and when it was the jay that came,
the dog stopped panting
and tried to look alert.
And when it was the cat advancing,
the dog began her steady breath.
Nothing was established while we waited,

and the big stillness on our left went on.
And on our right, motion and commotion
in the shade, sound and action, seats
on a seesaw neither would abandon.

Swissed

I had inadvertently stepped on the heel of the girl in front of me and she had walked right out of her shoe. Which was to us hilarious, largely because it disturbed the solemnity of single file and made a daring little joke on the oft-repeated phrase, *hands to yourselves*. Admittedly, we did giggle and bunch up, and I was singled out and put in front, making memory clearer. The plain beige linoleum, despite its stubborn scuff marks, gleamed. I so wanted to mock the walk of our teacher now that I'd been made an isolate, put in a category all of my own: neither teacher nor student now, but one wanting discipline. The cheese stands alone, I was feeling that. I could feel the little wind through the holes.

Trail

idea   Maybe it was the arrival of the secular breeze, the
               emergence,
        in other words, of weather in Eden
        that gave them the idea to clothe themselves.
        Not a wicked wind, not a just wind. Just wind.

dream   Everything had been cleared away: the gravel pile, the
               railings and sheet metal,
        the flower stalls, their blooms and grasses,
        and other businesses where once we'd expected to find what
               we needed
        arranged very near to what we'd discover we wanted:
        extension cords and Chinese handcuffs,
        assorted cheeses, brooms, jars of black olives in brine.

        There were the emptied racks remaining, a stack of bins.

real   I stepped off the trail and reached for a horsetail at the stage
               of its sporing.
        I love this plant, and when I called out to you, I felt the
               vibration through the stem.
        And when I was quiet then, the movement continued in the
               stem.
        I let go, and presume that it stopped.

III

Accord

Outside a window of the dining hall, rain continued evenly
even as the next pane
framed the weather of the rain's completion.

Since weather is a local thing and mobile, it has to have edges.
This has to happen somewhere all the time, I said,
so why do we never

or seldom see the two states side by side like this?
and why do we wait so patiently and long for something else?
I was lucky to be looking up.

Tell how the others entered then, a little late, and pulled us out.
It was urgent to them that we come.
Such a specimen—doubled and full spectrum—

assembled then and there
above the bridge we daily crossed to do our work.
The drops were cold. The river shook.

Johnson, Vermont

The Vacuum

Don't ask what it was all about.
Ask instead how sudden it was, how complete.
One minute I was an ordinary woman
vacuuming, a thing it seemed I had too recently done,
and the next minute sobbing,
emitting sounds loud, rapid, and long.
It was the kind of sobbing that makes you feel five—
five years old, or housing a feeling five people wide.
I was seated, my left elbow on my left knee,
my glasses hanging from my left hand
as if they were the problem
(no use in wearing them, no use in putting them down),
and the vacuum, part pet, part sculpture,
sprawled awkwardly, still shrieking
on the floor in front of me.
The sorrow seemed pulled from outside, unselectively,
as if I had swallowed a magnet.
Each time I felt that I could silence this,
that something had been spent, something settled,
I opened my eyes to that canister,
attachments on its back, hose, and extension,
reality-piece which had withstood the worst of me,
had witnessed, and was unaffected.

A Mile In

The snow had been with us for a while
and was dingy and not well lit.
But the sun promised to come out.
The light fog lifting
against the skinny tree trunks
and the grounded limbs they'd lost
and the thick, half-detached vines
would dissipate,
dissolved, by the end of our walk.
We'd taken the footbridge
across the creek and followed the bend
away from traffic and toward the west ridge.
We'd gone a mile in,
to where usually I begin to listen to
our progress in the twigs and gravel of the path,
and past this, and past my own
periodic reminders to the dog
to the short, uncomplicated songs
of winter birds. And there,
near the spill of rocks in the creek
where the fog was still passing through branches
and a little farther and to the right
where a stretch of tall grasses
received a wide gift
of sunlight and several cows,
the air that stood still
between the trees and shimmered
over the grasses filled with sound —
a big voice moving through
a hundred thousand habitats —

and it said, "Attention in this area.
The following is a regular monthly
test of the Outdoor Warning System . . ."
It spoke from the west first,
sounding closer than it could be.
And it spoke from the southeast next.
"This is a test," it said, "only a . . .
"This is a test . . . " it began again
from somewhere else.
The dog returned to me, cowering.
I'd wondered before
without much curiosity,
where were those speakers housed,
were they towered, did they revolve?
Ordinarily heard in the yard
while I stood pinning laundry to the line,
the broadcast soon plunged and sank
into the noise of passing cars
and blown and rolling garbage cans
and faded like the little ringing
that emanates from construction sites.
But here, it seemed full minutes long
before my breath was back again in my chest,
and my dog's breath,
steady and rough, was back in hers,
when the voice had left the air
between the trees, as had the fog.
At last a bird sounded from a twig.
At last a squirrel came down
and sent the dog. And then,
made up of other sounds
I could not have singled out,
a normalcy rolled in.
Infinitesimal bits is all it was
—quick beaks breaking up the peat,

the slow collision of a leaf landing, scooting
half an inch along a big flat rock,
a splat of excrement in white,
a flinch, a flap, a flick. But as it came it felt
to be a counter-vigilance. Or like
the sound of consciousness. The is.

McCall's 8041

Lay the pattern pieces on the cloth
to radio reports of the probable war.
What a blessing that the sleeve cap
takes up space exactly where
the front and back shirttails give some up.
Double-check before you cut. Walk
around it, to the other side of the table,
and read upside down what you've done.
Has the tiny lap-piece been forgotten?
Cut it with shears and mark with a wheel like a gear.
What a pleasure when you hear the needle
perforate a tightly woven cotton
after days of slippery crepe de chine
and then not to hear a thing as it sinks
into a double-soft oxford cloth
except the sound of speed and slacking speed
determined by the foot, the periodic
clack of fingernails or pins against
the metal plate as you lift and fold—so
quickly—a portion of the cloth, insisting
that a seam shall curve or narrow
imperceptibly or pirouette
at needle point to turn a corner square.

In the Garden of Dr. Sun Yat-Sen

I'd never seen bamboo like that:
living, green. I slipped between the stems,
weaving through them. Permission seemed
to come from something in their structure.
And through the lattice openings

in the wall between the gardens, I saw people
passing slowly, examining the vegetation
growing closest, or noticing
what had before been hidden from them.
In the garden of Dr. Sun Yat-Sen,

the paths have been allowed to modulate
in their materials—gray sunken pebbles,
then darker oblong stones—and curved tiles,
glazed and cooled to darkest brown,
reappear throughout the grounds:

as shingles on pavilion roofs and, worked
into the landscaping, there they are again,
set on edge and lining sections of the path,
establishing by increments
one tempered tone. Sometimes people

slowed, sometimes they stopped,
their postures settled, sinking,
and then this drifted down and caught:
it made no difference to them anymore
and never mind and let it drop,

although we couldn't help but hear
the air wound taut—bright white screamings
from the Molson Indy, near.
I'd glimpsed it from the sky train
just before our stop

when a man seated facing me
—twenty-eight he must have been,
Asian, in his business suit—straightened
in excitement and, smiling hard enough
to be a boy, lifted from his seat,

and lodged that moment into history.
In the garden of Dr. Sun Yat-Sen,
everyone walked through that noise,
or paused in it, as if it weren't unfortunate.
There, everything has been measured,

everything has been observed.
Long ago a gong was struck.
Sound shimmied through the air,
through bamboo, pine, and winter-blooming plum.
The sound was in the pond, the stones,

each leaf and space between, the sound was in
the wood plank sequence of the bridge.
The turtle on the rock held his head level
to that sound. He would never move.
The sound would never stop.

Vancouver, B.C.

Of

To think that we refer, still,
to the "ring" of the telephone—
as if it ever once made the circular sound
that comes from the shape of a bell.
And the brown of the leaves
fallen down from the oak
is closer to the color of the skin
on the back of my hands we call white—
what is the color now, is it brown?
The horizon in town will not let
the pure clear blue of the sky touch ground.
And so it is that children
instinctively restrict it
to a strip high up, made comical to us
because of the corner cut away for the sun.
The obligatory sun!
Of which just a pinch is limitless:
who can represent it with the crayons
in the standard set—that shine?
Even when it's all filled in,
the picture omits what was meant.
But the houses of childhood step up, large,
so forward on the page
that the lawns tucked under them thin,
putting the door of the house
as near as truth to us,
and, as an afterthought drawn over it,
the dark knob, slow-considered
and deliberate. As for proportion—
even when it slips a bit

and delivers the small-headed dog,
the boy with one ear larger,
the fence that bends and sends itself, not back,
but straight up, skyward, and looking like a ladder—
the longer we let it stay with us,
the less it looks far-fetched.

Early Cinematography

The cinema is an invention without a future.
—Louis Lumière

An elm by the side of the road.

An elm by the side of the road.

Was that a slight breeze
Lifting some of the leaves?

A wagon, pulled by a horse,
Appears, but there's been
No approach to speak of;

A wagon has entered the picture
Without a sound to signal it.
Nor can there be

Departure into distance
—O we have the will,
But not a way to follow it.

Our focus is fixed.
An elm by the side of the road.
A disturbance in the leaves . . .

Is this on a loop, have we
Seen the whole thing?

Possibility is constant.

Musée Lumière, Lyon

But All Energy Does Go Somewhere

Whatever you did with your afternoon,
I bet it was spent more successfully
than mine. I attempted to write a letter
of medium length to my mother.
Then, although I'd revised as I went—
deleting and substituting, thinking better
of mentioning one thing or another—
I spent the evening revising it again.
We don't actually know one another.

It had to be perfect.
No, it had to be engaging, it had to
instigate the wanting of more of the same.
It had to place in her heart
a contagion of curiosity.
It had to be about language more than life.
It had to be I don't care if you never answer this.
It had to declare my essence an innate
affiliate to hers. It had to prove to her
I came from her.
                    And yet, in truth,
it had no more obligation than a bench
I'd sat down on next to an old woman
I'd never met, never spoken to. Still,
it had to have something to say.
It was awkward. I wanted it to be natural
and smooth, fluent, easygoing, affable,
but smart. It was, perhaps, too much to
ask, one adjective too much to ask.

Indoor Tundra

The little that happens happens so slightly.
White and weightless,

but it does pile up. Every so often
a long slow spray of slush thrown out by a passing car
spills invisible glitter onto my shoulders

inside the house. I feel it, just barely, something
from long ago this same time of year,
something that ended just before dusk.

When I take a walk later on a day like this,
even if I am paired with my husband,
little will be spoken. We curl inside ourselves.

It is early December, snow-heavy, clouded.
The plows have been out
and they have honeycombed the slush.

A wrapped package under the arm,
and that sound, paper against a coat sleeve,
that's the sound this afternoon keeps making, close to me or far,

and then scatters the glitter again, invisibly.
As daylight capitulates and the telephone rings,
what is it that lifts a little, slightly disturbed,

and resettles slowly, unseen,
and as soundless as scrutiny? I have lost track
and can't say how slowly. Someone speaking into my ear

has become a conversation in a dining room gone dark
when someone at the side door rattles it and enters
and a finger rubbed against the wall lifts up

and the room is full of furniture.

In Which I Am Taken for a Ride

"Looks like I've got myself into trouble," I said
and was given, in lieu of reply,
a telltale sideways nod from someone I right then decided
must be another woman. The men
were in the front seat, and they weren't looking back.

The destination, it turned out,
was Mexico, although the drive itself—part of it with ocean
washing right across the road ahead of us,
part of it teetering high above the vast
unwinding view to our left—

as well as the train ride that followed—
we can't forget that!—
were so lengthy and elaborate
that I wondered at one point if we'd passed right through
Central America and were now on to something else . . .

Bolivia, Brazil, Guyana, Gabon. But that was later,
as we maneuvered our zigzag way
through the aisles of a large discount department store
that right at its center was hay-strewn, skylit,
and actually outdoors.

And how had I tangled myself up in this mess
in the first place? this seems the time to ask.
It comes back to me now
that my home had been sold, I'd figured something out,
I'd wandered off, down the road

only to be picked up by the carful
of foreign-seeming folk. Wedged in like that
with the women, I'd been talkative. I'd asked about
the heavy, dark, striped, handwoven cloth that covered them,
and I'd nattered on, probably revealing,

in the end, too much about myself. Whatever I'd said,
it was enough to hate me (or what I stood for) for,
it was enough to take me for a ride
from which I was unlikely ever to return
unless I could do so on my own, surreptitiously and soon.

When I asked the one I'd spoken to most—
the one I'd been seated next to in the car—
what her name was, she paused, and answered, "Julie."
I was told the other woman
also had that name. Although by whom has faded.

My Lifelong Relationship with God

We have not spoken for nearly thirty years.
It's difficult to remember the precise moment when something stops.
I tried to quit smoking so many times, for example,
that I don't know the date of my success.
I still like the same sensations I did as a girl in the 1950s.
Sun on my shoulder, a breeze on the nape of my neck.
Pulling the cotton laces of canvas shoes tight to tie them.
Losing myself in the thicket of a book.
The way my torso and limbs and neck feel after swimming.
Stirring with a wooden spoon. Hearing the wooden spoon
against the side of the bowl. Yards that invite a body
to run down the hill. Things that fit together.

Some did not want it to unfold as it did, but I came to be nonetheless.
We needn't grow quiet now.
We all have had plans that are canceled and plans that are not.
We all know that what disappoints isn't always due to us.
If replacing God with another phrase would work, I would do it.
It would not be love, however. It would not be God is Love.
God is Love is like trying to climb up a string instead of a ladder.
When I count my blessings, and they are many,
I consider them as much or as little my fault as anyone else's.
That it rains today, that I wrote something down,
that I was born in June when we have peas and lettuce
in the garden. If we have planted them. If we know how to do that.
If the yard has a garden. If a yard with a garden appealed
to our younger selves. If the groundhog has not found a way in.
If the owl in the oak does its work.

My Neighbor's Maple

If I were painting instead
I could reach for a red, a rust red,
that metallic.

I'd have to know how to silver it,
too, to suggest
what must be mist, but isn't.

It must be the time change, I think,
or the overcast day
closing down day

as if it were closer to evening
than it actually is
which it isn't.

No, it's done by the oaks,
I can see that now.
The oaks are the unspoken

presence behind this.
But now they have interest.
And there's new doubt in the air,

about the sun
coming out or not coming out,
exquisite with indecision.

Monday

I woke up listening. A sound was tunneling
through the air. Familiar and quaint—
industrial—it tumbled the outskirts,

curving past Bertram, then Otis Road,
blaring at markers, boulders, at gravel
or pavement at un-gated crossings,

spreading wide over parallel lines
of rail-bed grasses, over leftover lots
with Queen Anne's lace and black-eyed Susans,

and then the cleaner fields, the corn—
commandeered and obedient—
and it played through the structure of Cargill

and alongside the long sides of trucks
lined up to the left. And as it reached
the southernmost side of my city,

the nearby birds of my own yard had begun
to voice their intentions. I heard
and was each time surprised by

the space between notes, and by the space
between a cluster of notes and its next
occurrence. I knew enough not to turn over,

not to begin the day making coffee.
It seemed I'd been granted an aptitude
for deep passivity. I lay there,

picturing the species-non-specific
countenance of the last one to warble,
the head cocked in thought or reception

the way that birds do, nearly continually,
every few seconds. And some of the sound
had pooled, and new dots of sound

pocked the surface.
This could be a day like no other, I thought.
This could be a day like each one to follow,

and I imagined then a pleasant,
uneventful, string of such days,
indistinct and permeable,

like a vacation remembered after twenty years
as little more than tall reeds
and the sound of water lapping

something made of wood.
Knowing this in advance as we do,
why then is one tempted, on the day of departure,

on that final morning,
the day to slide the suitcase out from under the cot,
to turn to one's companion,

and unexpectedly say it, Look,
you go on ahead. I'll let you know later
what developed and how close it came

to perfection.

Now

The passage in the book,
Remarkable at first,
Has stepped back
Behind another.

The flame is not lit
And not put out;
The wick is white and what you
Would have said, unstated.

All the time in the world
Is the round, unmarked
Vase that a dealer
Has recently dusted.

Ocean

When the temperature exceeds 72°, I will wade farther in and swim,
I promised myself. So when, on the very next day, it did, I had to
brave it then.
And when I entered the ocean, the wind was strong and the waves
were high.
I had not at all prepared myself for the salt. Had I recalled the fact
in advance
that salt comes from our seas, I still would not have been ready to
receive it like that
—at such potency, I mean—in my nose, in my mouth. I sputtered
at first.
Soon enough, though, I was flat on my back, relaxed, as good as
adapted,
and just plain glad for my luck, *this is gorgeous, so warm—in*
September, no less!
But of course in time I stood up. Hardly had one uneventful
second passed
before I was startled by a crab, the tender and rarely-touched skin
on the top of my foot signaling trespass in this fashion:
ALERT, ALERT, something tickety and alive is currently crossing
the bridge!
But I recovered from that and attempted to swim as when I do laps
at the Y,
which I found to be unneeded, really, at this place and time.
So I bobbed and bicycled about and enjoyed the expanse.
When I returned to the towel where the beat of my heart
drummed into the sand,
I was dry within moments, my muscles relaxed and exhausted, and
I said to myself,
or possibly aloud in the quiet out-rushing form of a sigh, *This is*
most excellent,

which translates as follows: it is like I am lying here dead and
hyper-alive all at once,
lying here with profound passivity in the midst of big sound and
big sun
and the landing and leaving of waterfowl, and all of it is rhythmic as
I, too, am rhythmic
with my pulse-in-sand presence as well, and I can feel a tilting
going on here,
but its rhythms are bigger and louder and feel like forever;
in fact they encompass me now and will surpass me one day, and
how pleasing
it was once to imagine that they, at least they, will not end but will
be everlasting.

Notes

"Qu'est-ce qu'il y a?": The poem's title phrase is idiomatic French for "What's the matter?"

"They Are Widening the Road": According to the U.S. Census Bureau's International Data Base (https://www.census.gov/newsroom /stories/2019/world-population-day.html), the world population reached 7 billion in 2012, 7.5 billion on June 13, 2018, and new projections indicate that the 8 billion marker will be reached in 2025. The poem's sum of 6 billion, since it cannot possibly keep current, must stand as a marker.

"Eclipse on the Day of the Field Trip": The setting for this poem is Ushers Ferry Historic Village and Seminole Valley Farm in Cedar Rapids, Iowa, a popular field trip destination for elementary schoolchildren. On May 10, 1994, maximum eclipse (annular) was achieved at 12:11:28 p.m. at this location. The poem follows the activities of a class of fifth graders on that day, as observed by a parent volunteer.

"In the Garden of Dr. Sun Yat-Sen": This poem references the 2001 Molson Indy Vancouver Championship Auto Racing Teams (CART) motor race held on September 2, 2001, a Grand Prix–style course set to run through the blocked-off streets of the city. A segment of the course cut into Chinatown within blocks of the gardens that are the poem's setting.

"But All Energy Does Go Somewhere": The reader is invited to remember that some individuals are born to people who, for whatever reason, cannot afford to engage meaningfully with their new offspring and may need to decline the role of parenting them.

The children move off into alternate lives, possibly happy ones, and do not necessarily learn of the circumstances and cause for their surrender. Indeed, they may never know that it occurred.

Acknowledgments

Grateful acknowledgment is made to the editors of the following journals where these poems, or versions of them, first appeared:

"It is unconquerable; it has," *The Cincinnati Review*; "Re-entry," *Conduit*; "My Job as a Child" and "In the Garden of Dr. Sun Yat-Sen," *Crab Orchard Review*; "Law," "27 October. Dreary." and "Early Cinematography," *Diode*; "The Applicant's Wife's Rendering of the Facility Tour," *Fulcrum*; "Why Do Men Spit?" and "But All Energy Does Go Somewhere," *Great River Review*; "Eclipse on the Day of the Field Trip," *The Iowa Review*; "Final Moments, Summer School," *The Journal*; "Advent" and "Indoor Tundra," *Meridian*; "A Tan Dog Standing," *Michigan Quarterly Review*; "Qu'est-ce qu'il y a?" "The Vacuum," "A Mile In," and "My Lifelong Relationship with God," *New Ohio Review*; "The Clacklet," *Plume*; "At Pauline's" and "Dialectic and Infusion," *Poetry East*; "Rundown Ride," *Press*; "Squall Line Stalling in a Memory of Rain," *Salamander*; "Method," *Smartish Pace*; "They Are Widening the Road," *Terrain.org*; "The Prints from Vacation Are Back," *Two Rivers Review*; "The Meeting" and "Swissed," *VOLT*; "Now," *Water~Stone*; "Buttons" and "McCall's 8041," *West Branch*.

"Buttons" was republished with permission in the *Anthology of Magazine Verse & Yearbook of American Poetry*.

For timely recognition and generous gifts, I remain indebted to the National Endowment for the Arts, the Vermont Studio Center, and to Timothy Murphy and the Directors of the West Chester University Conference on Narrative and Form. I want to express my thanks as well to contest judge Nancy Eimers for finding "A Mile In" fit to be the winner of the 2011 *New Ohio Review* poetry contest and to *New Ohio Review* for the generous award.

I'm indebted to the several generations of my Iowa City writing group for serious consideration of these poems and of drafts long preceding these; for their own good examples of what can be done inside a poem; for the meetings themselves, in providing an excellent and compelling reason to generate work; and to the current members, especially, for their recent and ready counsel: Kathy Hall, David Hamilton, Dan Lechay, and Jan Weissmiller.

My thanks go again and again to Hollis Summers Poetry Prize contest judge Maggie Smith for selecting my manuscript and for finding merit in it. Her commendation is, and will remain, treasured. I'm glad for the luck and pleasure of working with Hollis Summers Poetry Prize series editor David Sanders on his final round, and for the continuing luck and pleasure of working with everyone at Ohio University Press. For the beautiful cover design, my wholehearted thanks to Beth Pratt, and for permissions generously granted, the Reynolda House Museum of American Art and the Charles E. Burchfield Foundation.

I am grateful for Rich and William Hanson, who have steadied and sustained me, who have inspired me, and laughed. Without their valuable companionship, without the fortunate accidents of our lives together, many of these poems would simply not have come about. I'm grateful again to Rich for his constant availability and unwavering curiosity as first listener to drafts of these poems, and whose most critical response, rarely given and relatively easy to receive, is the kind and telling blank look of expectancy. This is surprisingly instructive!

Finally, thank you to Mackie Rice, whose astute observations on the activity of reading initiated a valued episode in our correspondence that led me playfully to the title of the first poem in this collection, which, in turn, led to the poem beneath it.